W9-AHH-059

MAZES
AROUND THE WORLD

BY Mary D. Lankford ▣ ILLUSTRATED BY Karen Dugan

Collins
An Imprint of HarperCollinsPublishers

SCHENECTADY COUNTY
PUBLIC LIBRARY

GIFT

Collins is an imprint of HarperCollins Publishers.

Mazes Around the World
Text copyright © 2008 by Mary D. Lankford
Illustrations copyright © 2008 by Karen Dugan

Manufactured in China. All rights reserved. No part of this book may be used or reproduced in any manner whatsoever without written permission except in the case of brief quotations embodied in critical articles and reviews. For information address HarperCollins Children's Books, a division of HarperCollins Publishers, 1350 Avenue of the Americas, New York, NY 10019.
www.harpercollinschildrens.com

Library of Congress Cataloging-in-Publication Data is available.
ISBN-10: 0-688-16519-2 (trade bdg.) — ISBN-13: 978-0-688-16519-2 (trade bdg.)
ISBN-10: 0-688-16520-6 (lib. bdg.) — ISBN-13: 978-0-688-16520-8 (lib. bdg.)

Typography by Sarah Hoy
1 2 3 4 5 6 7 8 9 10
❖
First Edition

CONTENTS

6

Author's Note

I had the idea for this book when I was on an airplane, reading a magazine article on mazes and labyrinths. When I read that the history of mazes and labyrinths has been traced all the way back to Egyptian and Roman times, I was hooked. I went on a research hunt as soon as I got home. I wanted to learn more about the history and mystery of these timeless puzzles.

Through books, magazines, and the Internet, I learned about labyrinth patterns drawn on rocks and cave walls that had similarities repeated from continent to continent. I discovered stories told in mythology that helped explain why labyrinths were built and the superstitions that surrounded them. I examined photographs of beautiful gardens with hedges shaped into huge mazelike puzzles.

I learned that the words *maze* and *labyrinth* often mean the same thing. However, today a labyrinth is often thought of as a maze with a single path to the center, while a maze has many false turns and dead ends.

I enjoy writing about the similar games played in countries around the world. Researching mazes and labyrinths, I again marveled at how people of different cultures developed ideas, legends, traditions, and games that reflect common needs and interests. I found that mazes and labyrinths have varied purposes. I hope to share some of these discoveries with you. Let's take a look at some interesting ones built throughout history.

EGYPT: ANCIENT MAZES

Herodotus, a famous Greek writer, traveler, and historian, visited the Egyptian Labyrinth in the fifth century B.C. After a seven-day journey up the Nile from the Pyramids of Giza, he saw a vast, remarkable structure on the shores of Lake Moeris. It was a temple composed of twelve courts, all built of immense stone slabs and connected by passages so winding that visitors required a guide. Awestruck, Herodotus wrote, "I visited this building and found it to surpass description; for if all the great works of the Greeks could be put together in one, they would not equal this labyrinth. The pyramids likewise surpass description, but the labyrinth surpasses the pyramids." The amazing structures Herodotus referred to when praising the Egyptian Labyrinth included the Great Pyramid of Khufu, built in 2600 B.C., and the Parthenon, built in 477 B.C.!

Herodotus was not allowed to visit the lower levels of the complex, but he wrote that they contained the sepulchers, sometimes called tombs or burial vaults, of the kings who built the labyrinth.

The Egyptian Labyrinth was 1,300 years old when Herodotus visited it, and probably already in a state of disrepair. As time passed, the structure further eroded. In 1888, the British archaeologist Flinders Petrie excavated the site. All he found was an enormous field of chipped stone, six feet deep. Petrie surmised that it was evidence of a grand building but wrote, "From such very scanty remains it is hard to settle anything."

Not long after, much of the remaining stone was removed and used as bedding under railway lines. Almost nothing now remains of the spectacular structure once said to be even greater than the pyramids.

GREECE: THE MINOTAUR'S MAZE

Greek mythology tells of a monster with the body of a man and the head of a bull. This monster was the captive of King Minos, who ruled the Greek island of Crete. Minos had his master architect, Daedalus, build a huge labyrinth in an underground space at Knossos, a city on Crete. The hideous monster—the Minotaur—was kept inside this labyrinth, which had many confusing twists and dead ends.

After King Minos fought and defeated a rival monarch, King Aegeus of Greece, he demanded that King Aegeus provide a sacrifice to the Minotaur. Every nine years King Aegeus was forced to send seven young boys and seven young girls from Athens to Crete as a sacrifice. The young people would become lost in the maze of the labyrinth. Unable to find their way out, they were eventually eaten by the Minotaur.

One day the son of King Aegeus, Theseus, volunteered to be sent as a sacrifice. His plan was to kill the Minotaur and put an end to the deaths of young Athenians. As Theseus entered the maze, he unrolled a ball of golden twine behind him. According to the legend, Theseus fought and killed the Minotaur—and then escaped from the labyrinth by following the trail of twine.

Although the tale of Theseus and the Minotaur is a myth, ancient coins have been found in Knossos that depict the labyrinth pattern. And labyrinth designs are frequently seen on Cretan ceramic fragments that are now displayed in museums.

FRANCE: RELIGIOUS LABYRINTHS

You may be wondering about the difference between the words *maze* and *labyrinth*. In the story of Theseus and the Minotaur, and throughout history, the terms are used interchangeably. However, the labyrinth connected with religion and spirituality is a unicursal, or one-path, maze. This path leads to a large center area and continues on out of the maze. You cannot get lost in a unicursal maze, or labyrinth. The journey through a labyrinth has been compared to the journey of a life guided by faith, and the labyrinth has been used for religious purposes. Because you cannot get lost in a labyrinth, walking it provides comfort and a chance to meditate while moving safely along. People often stop at the center to reflect and pray before continuing along the path to its end.

The earliest known example of a labyrinth in a church is at El Asnam in Algeria, in the church of St. Reparatus. This labyrinth, thought to date from A.D. 324, is designed in black and white tile.

During the Middle Ages, many Christians vowed to go on a pilgrimage to the holy city of Jerusalem once during their life. But bandits and other dangers made such a trip too treacherous for most people, so labyrinths became a substitute for the pilgrimage. Christians would travel to a cathedral where a labyrinth had been built and walk the path, often on their knees, as a symbolic way to complete their journey. The walk to the center of the labyrinth was called the Road to Jerusalem.

One of the most famous of the medieval religious labyrinths can still be seen at Chartres Cathedral in France. Modern unicursal labyrinths, such as the one in San Francisco's Grace Cathedral, draw approximately two hundred thousand visitors a year.

SWEDEN: STONE MAZES

Stone labyrinths are commonly found near coastlines, particularly in parts of Scandinavia, including Sweden. Some historians believe that sailors built these mazes in order to calm strong winds by trapping the wind in the stones.

Walking to the center of a stone labyrinth and back out without stumbling is thought to bring good luck. In some parts of Sweden, fishermen walked a labyrinth before checking their nets for holes. In the southwest region of Sweden, shepherd boys walked the labyrinth as protection against wolves—believing that the wolves would be confused by the twisting path. This tradition was also followed in Lapland in hopes of protecting the reindeer herds.

Another tradition tells of Swedish fishermen walking mazes to prevent pesky trolls—imaginary small, mischievous beings—from accompanying them. In this example, the fishermen would enter the maze slowly with the trolls presumably following. Then the fishermen would run out and jump in their boats, leaving the trolls puzzled and trapped inside the maze.

These northern European stone structures are called *Trojbergs*, or Troy towns. They are found on islands or along the coast and are situated without being buried in the ground. Most Troy towns are found in Scandinavia, with approximately 300 in Sweden and another 141 in Finland.

UNITED KINGDOM: TURF MAZES

A turf maze is a raised path of grass made by digging out the soil on either side of the path, although sometimes it is reversed and the path is cut into the turf. Turf mazes are most associated with England, where they have been a tradition for centuries. Similar patterns have also been found in Germany.

In the Middle Ages turf mazes were widespread over the English countryside. Frequently located near churches, the patterns may have been borrowed from France after England was invaded by the Norman conquerors in 1066. Shakespeare mentions mazes in his play *A Midsummer Night's Dream*, when the fairy queen Titania says,

"And the quaint mazes in the wanton green
For lack of tread are undistinguishable."

(act 2, scene 1)

Maze-making became a fad in the late sixteenth century. Unlike the labyrinths created for religious purposes, these mazes are meant to confuse and amuse. Multicursal, with many paths that lead in the wrong direction or end abruptly, they test people's cleverness. It is easy to get lost in a multicursal maze.

Treading the Maze was a favorite game: a girl would stand alone in the center of the maze while the young men of the village tried to reach her first. This game sounds simple, but was more difficult when the players were blindfolded! Puritans disapproved of such frivolous activity and banned all maze games by law in an attempt to suppress "those folysche [sic] ceremonies."

Like stone labyrinths, turf mazes are also sometimes called Troy towns. In Wales they are called *Caerdroia*, which can mean "city of Troy."

UNITED KINGDOM: HEDGE MAZES

Although hedge mazes were once very popular across Europe—they were also found in Italy, France, Belgium, and Spain—today they are most commonly associated with the United Kingdom. Hedge mazes are also called puzzle mazes and have many dead ends and wrong turns. People enjoy finding the way out of the pattern.

Thousands of people visit mazes each year at historic sites in England such as Blenheim Palace, Longleat, and Leeds Castle. The maze at Leeds Castle in Kent involved the planting of three thousand yew trees. It has a unique centerpiece in the form of an underground grotto that is decorated with statues and fountains and has a ninety-foot-long secret passage. The maze makes Leeds Castle one of Britain's top tourist attractions.

The Hampton Court Palace maze, probably the most famous of all, entertains about six hundred thousand people every year. This maze is located near the Hampton Court Palace by the River Thames on the outskirts of London. It covers a third of an acre and is in almost exactly the same shape it was when it was built more than three hundred years ago. Can you imagine the secret meetings held in the Hampton Court Palace maze over the centuries?

Perhaps the largest permanent hedge maze is the Peace Maze at Castlewellan Forest Park in Northern Ireland. It covers 2,771 acres! Meanwhile, one of the longest hedge mazes in the world is at Longleat House in Bath, England. It opened to the public in 1978 and has a path of 1.69 miles.

Some hedge mazes are laid out in spectacular, fantastic designs. Famed maze designer Adrian Fisher created the Darwin Maze, which is located at the Scotland Zoo in Edinburgh. Seen from above, it looks like a giant Galapagos tortoise.

Adding water to a maze increases the challenge of finding one's way! A very famous water maze exists in England at Hever Castle.

This is a simple circular water maze with stepping-stones that lead to a central grotto. As you walk through the maze, stepping on the wrong stones causes you to be sprayed with a fountain of water coming from underneath the stone. But if you walk on the correct stones, you will not get wet. The quest ends at the center of the maze as you travel through a small grotto and up into a small tower that overlooks the entire maze.

Hever Castle's most famous inhabitant was Anne Boleyn, the second wife of Henry VIII in the 1500s. However, Anne never explored the water maze, because it was not added to the castle grounds until 1987.

Another recently built water maze is found at Victoria Park in Bristol, Avon, England. It was built in 1984, and although people cannot "walk" it, visitors can participate by floating a leaf or a twig along its twists and turns. In design it is a modern example of the labyrinth at Chartres.

Yet another water and hedge labyrinth may be found at the Château de Thoiry in France. This maze is shaped like a giant eye. A five-pointed star represents the five senses. There are nine bridges in the maze.

NORTH AMERICA: WOVEN MAZES

Some Native Americans used the labyrinth as a pattern for baskets. The Pima, who were known as "the basket weavers," have a strong labyrinth tradition. Museums have examples of hand-woven baskets decorated with an unusual nine-path variation of the classical seven-path design.

A Pima legend tells of Iitoi (the "Elder Brother"), a good man who was saved when a flood destroyed the world. Iitoi became the father of the Pima and of the Tohono O'otam people. When Iitoi was killed, his spirit escaped to a maze of paths where no one could follow. Hence, the Pima basket design is also known as the House of Iitoi. This labyrinth represents the many twists and turns of life.

The Hopi is another southwestern group of Native Americans with a labyrinth tradition. It is believed that the Hopi pueblo in Arizona was built in 1100 or 1200. It may be one of the oldest continuously inhabited places in North America. There are six labyrinth carvings just outside the pueblo. These Hopi designs, like some of the European labyrinths we have seen, have spiritual meaning and significance: they are thought to have represented *tapu'a* (mother and child), a sacred element in Hopi tradition. It is fascinating to see how the labyrinth is revered as a spiritual symbol around the world.

NORTH AMERICA: MAIZE MAZES

Maize mazes are enormously popular—but temporary.

Maize, also known as corn, is a cereal grain that was domesticated in Mesoamerica, a region extending south and east from central Mexico to include parts of Guatemala, Belize, Honduras, and Nicaragua. It spread to the rest of the world after European contact with the Americas in the late fifteenth and early sixteenth centuries.

Planting a seasonal corn maze is a newfound way for farmers to increase the income from their farms. During the growing season, the cornstalks provide barriers to sight and boundaries for the pattern. Maize mazes last for about two months before they are harvested for the corn. Exploring them is part of fall fun for many families. Renowned maze architect Adrian Fisher successfully designs maize mazes around the world but particularly in the United States each year.

Maize mazes are frequently planted in fantastic patterns that look spectacular when viewed from the air. One Arizona maze used three hundred thousand cornstalks to depict a Mayan sun symbol fashioned into the shape of Arizona. Another corn maze, located in Pennsylvania, was shaped like the Liberty Bell, while a Delaware maze re-created the famous painting of George Washington crossing the Delaware River.

SOUTH AFRICA: SOEKERSHOF MAZES

South Africa is located at the southernmost tip of the African continent. It is a beautiful country that has more than twenty thousand different plant species—about 10 percent of all known plant species on earth!

The Soekershof Walkabout in South Africa is home to lush gardens and one of the world's largest multicursal hedge mazes, the Klaas Voogds Maze. The word *Soekershof* is Afrikaans for "seeker's court."

The Klaas Voogds Maze is built of fourteen different varieties of hedge shrubs, including the tecomaria and the hibiscus, which flower year-round. This maze also incorporates two cacti labyrinths.

The Klaas Voogds is a maze of stories. The stories, based on local folklore, are depicted with objects towering above the hedges.

Another maze, the Langeberg, has patches of indigenous (veld) plants, partly native to the Klaas Voogds area and the Langeberg Mountains. It is also a succulent garden with more than fifteen hundred different succulents and cacti in the open air.

Thus, visiting the Soekershof Walkabout is a true tropical experience!

FUN WITH MAZES

Translations for *Maze* and *Labyrinth*

NEDERLANDS (Dutch)

labyrint

PORTUGUÊS (Portuguese)

labirinto

FRANÇAIS (French)

labyrinthe

ESPAÑOL (Spanish)

laberinto

DEUTSCH (German)

labyrinth

SVENSKA (Swedish)

labyrint

ITALIANO (Italian)

labirinto

BIBLIOGRAPHY

Artress, Lauren, Dr. *Walking a Sacred Path: Rediscovering the Labyrinth as a Spiritual Tool*. New York: Riverhead Books, 1995.

Bertman, Stephen. *Doorways Through Time: The Romance of Archaeology*. Los Angeles: Jeremy P. Tarcher, 1986.

Coomaraswamy, Amanda K. "The One Thread." *The Iconography of Durer's Knots and Leonardo's Concatenation*. Detroit: Detroit Institute of Arts: *Art Quarterly*, vol. VII, no. 2, 1944: 26–33.

Davis, Brian. "Room to Roam Between the Ears." *The Dallas Morning News*, 1 Sept. 2002, sec. Texas & Southwest: 43–44.

DeVries, Hilary. "Oases of Serenity East and West." *The New York Times*, 30 Dec. 2001, sec. 5: 1,7.

Fernandi, Kelly. "Minotaurmaze Exhibits." *Minotaur Maze Exhibits*, 30 Jan. 2006. http://www.minotaurmazes.com

Fisher, Adrian, and Howard Loxton. *Secrets of the Maze: An Interactive Guide to the World's Most Amazing Mazes*. London: Quarto Publishing, 1977.

Iowa State University. "Maize: Gift from America's First Peoples." *The Maize Page*. Iowa State University, 30 Jan. 2006. http://maize.agron.iastate.edu/

Kern, Hermann. *Through the Labyrinth*. Munich: Prestel Verlag, 2000.

Kirby, Robert. "It's Corny, but Maize Maze Lots of Fun." *The Salt Lake Tribune*, 23 Sept. 1999: C1.

Matthews, W. H. *Mazes and Labyrinths: Their History and Development*. 1922. New York: Dover Publications, 1970.

McCullough, David Willis. *The Unending Mystery: A Journey Through Labyrinths and Mazes*. New York: Pantheon Books, 2004.

Meehan, Aidan. "Chapters II, III, V, VI." *Maze Patterns (Celtic Design)*. London: Thames & Hudson, 1994. 34–35, 42–53, 72–79, 88–99, 114–115.

"Oahu's Dle Plantation More A-mazing Than Ever." *San Francisco Examiner*, 14 May 2000: T–3.

Orcutt, Larry. "The Ancient Egyptian Labyrinth." *Catchpenny Mysteries*, 27 Jan. 2006. www.catchpenny.org

Phillips, Tony. "Through Mazes to Mathematics." *SAT Mazes*. Math Dept., SUNY, Stony Brook, 5 June 1999. http://www.math.sunysb.edu/~tony/mazes

Price, Eluned E. "The Eternal Maze." *House Beautiful*, Dec. 1995: 76–81.

Salvador, Ricardo J. "The Maize Page." *The Encyclopedia of Mexico: History, Culture and Society. The Maize Page*. 1997. Iowa State University, Agronomy Department, 30 Jan. 2006. http://maize.agron.iastate.edu/

Thacker, Christopher. *The Genius of Gardening: The History of Gardens in Britain and Ireland*. London: Weidenfeld and Nicolson, 1994.

INDEX

X